Lecuona's Best Made Easier for You

An album of his foremost piano solos

CONTENTS

EDWARD B.
MARKS MUSIC
COMPANY

EXCLUSIVELY DISTRIBUTED BY

HAL•LEONARD®
CORPORATION
7777 W. BLUEMOUND RD. P.O. BOX 13819 MILWAUKEE, WI 53213

MALAGUEÑA

From the Spanish Suite "ANDALUCIA"

By ERNESTO LECUONA

Transcription by
GREGORY STONE

Allegro moderato

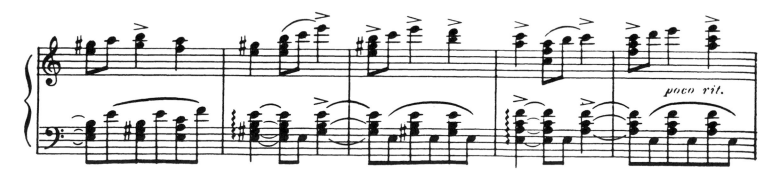

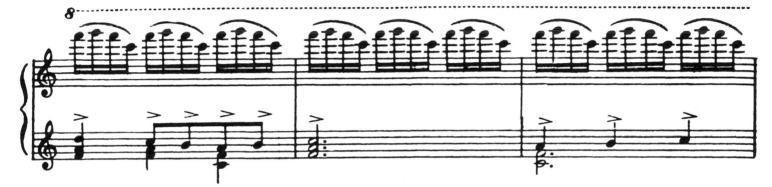

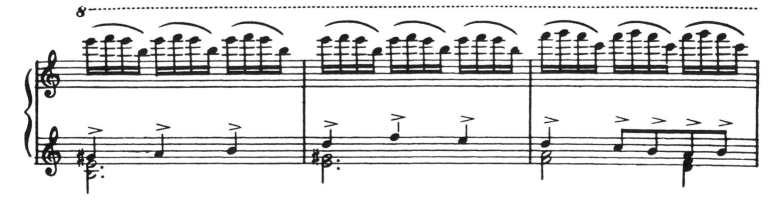

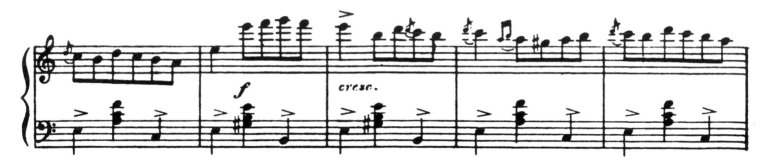

ANDALUCIA

FROM

(ANDALUCIA SUITE)

Arranged By
LOUIS SUGARMAN

By
ERNESTO LECUONA

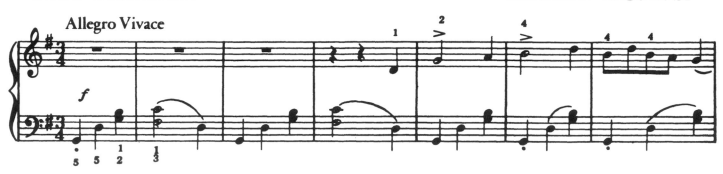

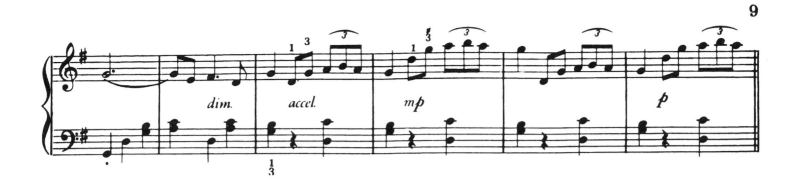

Molto Vivace

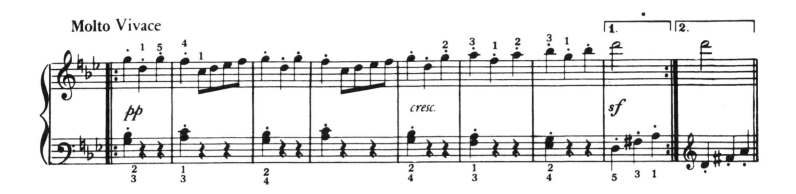

Allegro Vivace

LA COMPARSA
(Carnival Procession)

Transcription by
'LOUIS SUGARMAN

ERNESTO LECUONA

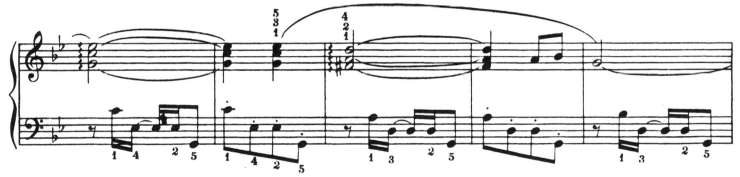

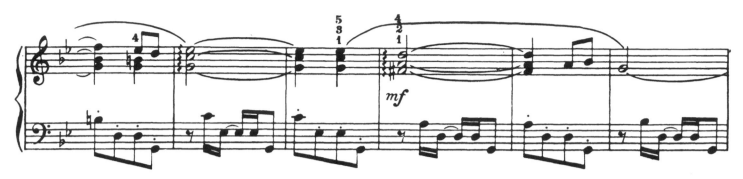

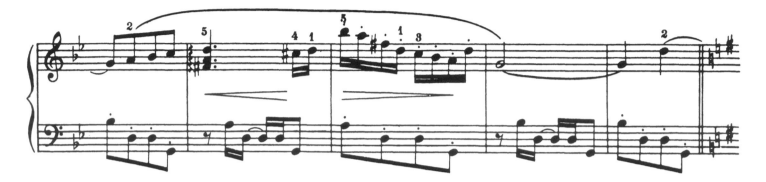

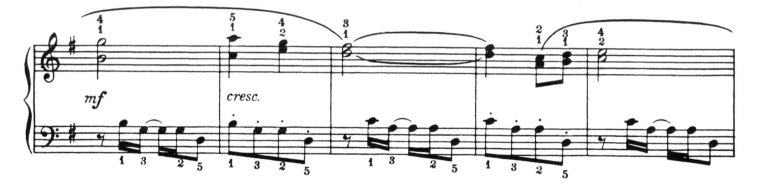

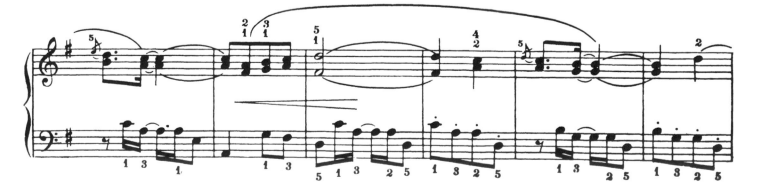

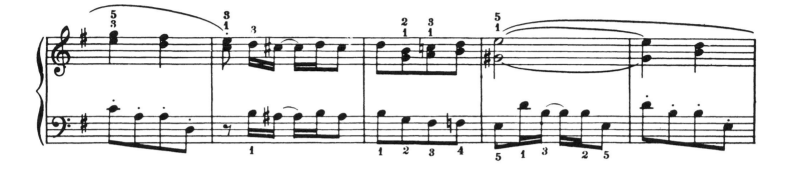

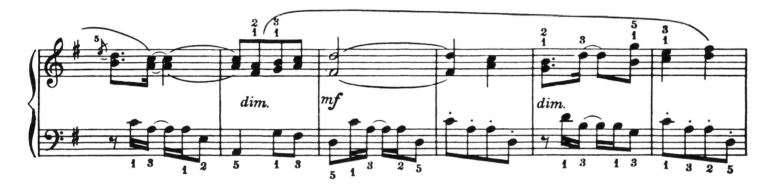

GITANERIAS
From "Andalucia Suite"

Transcription by
LOUIS SUGARMAN

ERNESTO LECUONA

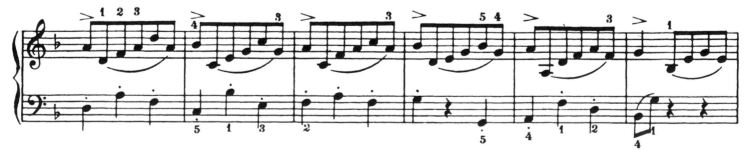

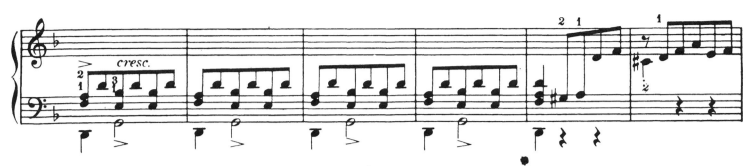

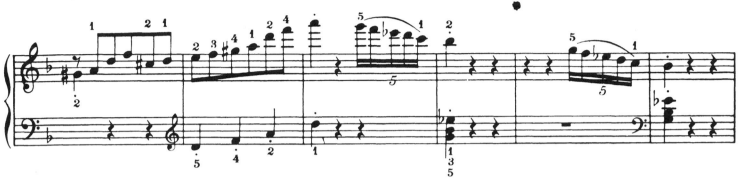

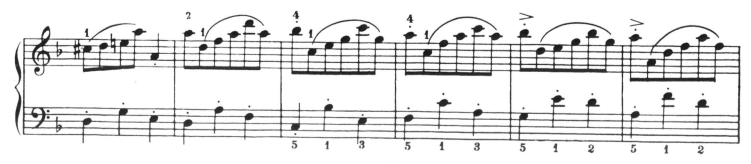

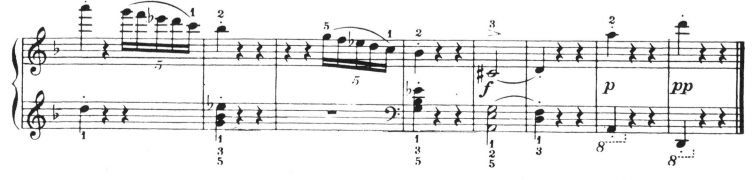

CORDOBA
from "ANDALUCIA" Suite

Simplified Arrangement by
LOUIS SUGARMAN

ERNESTO LECUONA

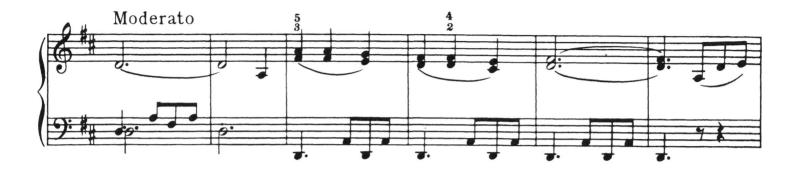

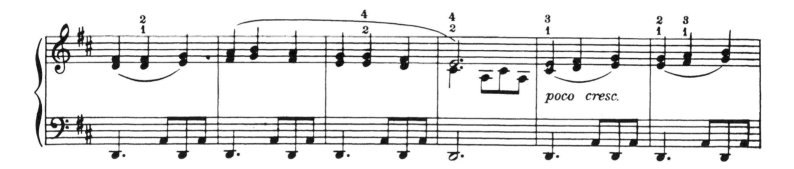

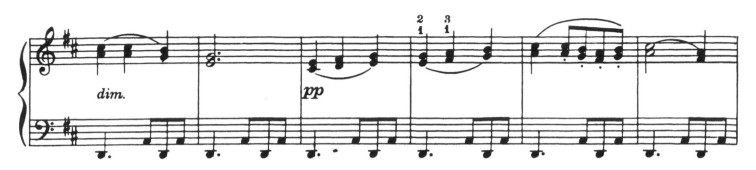

DANZA LUCUMI

from "DANZAS AFRO-CUBANAS" Suite

Simplified Arrangement by
LOUIS SUGARMAN

ERNESTO LECUONA

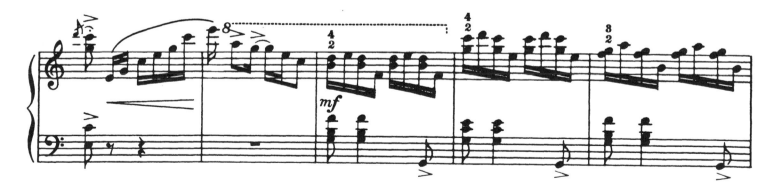

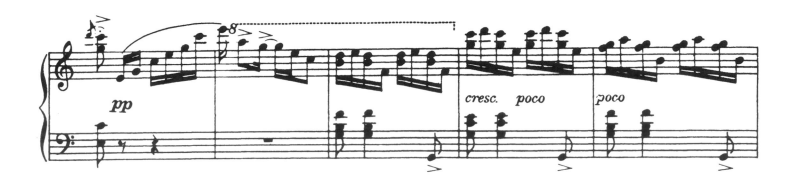

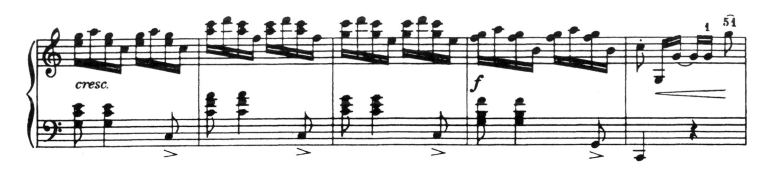

ANTE EL ESCORIAL

**Arranged by
LOUIS SUGARMAN**

ERNESTO LECUONA

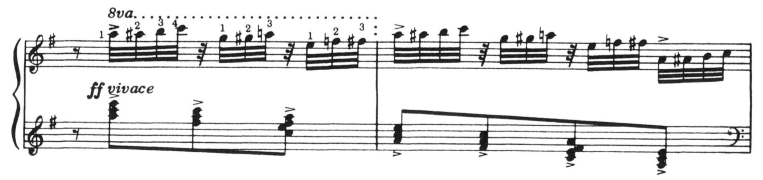

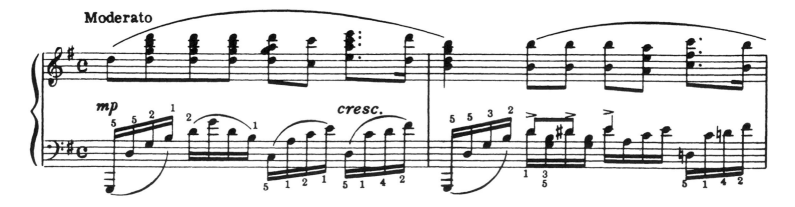

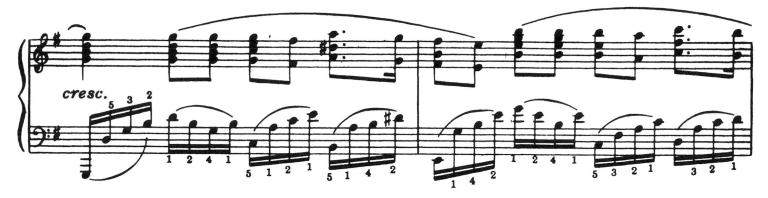

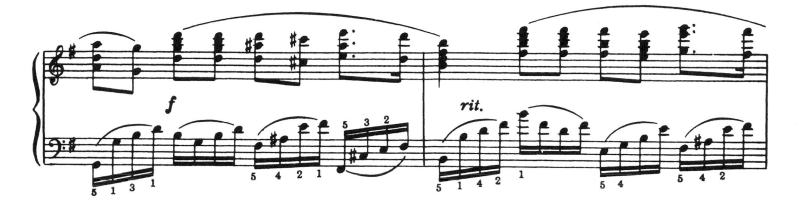

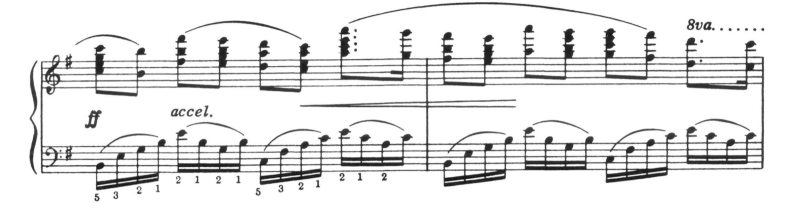

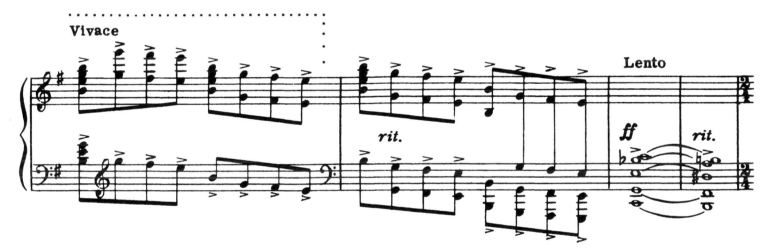

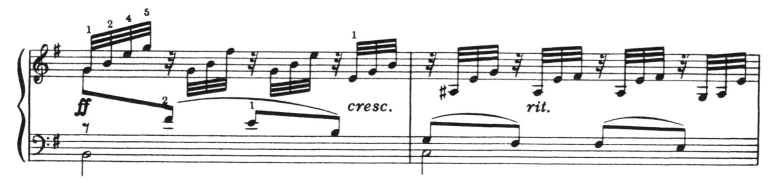

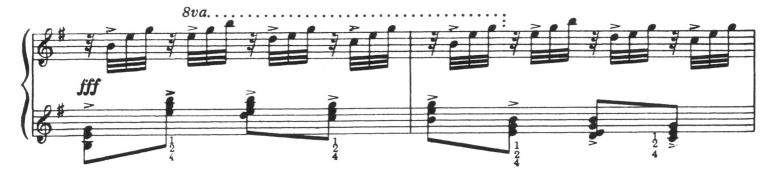